The Counterpunch Series

A Flight Manual for Prospective Angels

Join the Flight!

JOE NOLAND

HOPE: *A Flight Manual for Prospective Angels*
published by Hope Productions, Inc.

© 2004 by Joe Noland

Cover design by John Megowan; book design by Lily Chen

Scripture quotations are from:

Contemporary English Version (CEV)
©1991,1992, 1995 by American Bible Society.
Used by permission.

New King James Version (NKJV)
© 1979, 1980, 1982 by Thomas Nelson, Inc., Publishers.
Used by permission.

The Living Bible (TLB)
© 1971 by Tyndale House Publishers, Wheaton, IL.
Used by permission.

ALL RIGHTS RESERVED
No part of this publication may be reproduced, stored in a
retrieval system, or transmitted, in any form or by any means—
electronic, mechanical, photocopying, recording, or otherwise—
without prior written permission.

For information:
Hope Productions
P.O. Box 1690
Yucaipa, California 92399

www.jointheflight.com

TABLE OF CONTENTS

Preface 7

Introduction..9

Section One   HOPE! The Flight Plan 11

Section Two   HELL! The Blight Path 39

Section Three HELP! The Plight Pattern 57

Section Four   HOPE! The Flight Plan (Amplified) ..77

Epilogue..113

Dedicated to all "intervening earth angels"—
past, present and future—who have made a
"future changing" difference in the life
of a child.

***

My thanks and gratitude to Linda Johnson
and her staff in the Literary Department of
The Salvation Army, USA Eastern Territory.
Extraordinary!

Our Lord, you will always rule,

but nations will vanish from the earth.

You listen to the longings of those who suffer.

You offer them hope,

and you pay attention to their cries for help.

You defend orphans and everyone else in need.

–Psalm 10:16-18a *(CEV)*

Preface

Robert grew up in one of the most affluent sections of America: Orange County, California. He was a young boy in the late 70s when mega–churches were beginning to sprout like wildflowers across that Southern California landscape. Following Robert Schuller's lead, the burgeoning churches of Orange County were soon to form the "Bible Belt" of the West.

It was during this spiritually charged time and in the shadow of those cross–topped towers that Robert entered his formative years, critical years that would shape, mold, and pattern his value systems. Unfortunately, he was not off to a good start. In the midst of unprecedented affluence, Robert knew only poverty. In the shadows of this church growth phenomenon, he felt only loneliness and a sense of hopelessness. Abuse and neglect wove the fabric of his young life. Even in the prosperous, protected suburbs of Orange County, Robert was at high risk of succumbing to the seemingly irresistible forces of peer pressure and gang violence.

Several years earlier, at the age of five, Robert had been recruited into the Golden West Gang. In his own words, "Gangs usually like to recruit young kids because cops don't suspect them. And even if they do get arrested, they won't do any jail time." His life was beginning to spiral in a dangerous direction.

Robert desperately needed an intervening angel. Would that angel appear? Could you have been that angel in his life or in the life of a child facing similar circumstances? Did Robert ever find his angel?

INTRODUCTION

This is a flight manual for prospective angels of the temporal kind—earth angels. You might even want to view this as an angel–apprenticeship program, one that may eventually find its fulfillment in the heavenly realm. Any way you want to look at it, this manual is meant to be the catalyst that will inspire, motivate, train, and mobilize an army of angels ready and willing to put their lives on the line for a better future.

This manual is about protecting our children. It's about shaping the future through intervention and prevention. It's about opportunity, risk and change. It's about the blight on this planet and the plight of our children. It's about a revolutionary flight plan that will take us to new heights morally, ethically, and spiritually. It's about you and one of the most important decisions you will ever make. Above all, it's about hope—and a promise from God of prosperity.

HOPE!
THE FLIGHT PLAN

For I know the plans I have for you, says the Lord. They are plans for good and not for evil, to give you a future and a hope.
—*Jeremiah 29:11 (The Living Bible)*

What a promise! The Lord wants to give you a two-fold blessing, for Goodness sake! He wants to prosper you, and He wants to prosper the future through you. Earlier, in verse 7, the prophet Jeremiah writes, "Also seek the peace and prosperity of the city … Pray to the Lord for it, because if it prospers, you too will prosper." Can you grasp the implications of this promise—for you personally?

The message of Scripture is for all generations and can be applied to each unique circumstance. The prophet wrote this letter to God's people living in Babylon, a blighted city. And the Lord was telling His people to seek and pray for the peace and prosperity of the city—"because if it prospers, you too will prosper."

We must understand how God uses the word *prosper* in this situation. It must be interpreted in a spiritual context. Its root meaning is found in the Hebrew word *shalom*, which suggests "health, prosperity, and peace." At the time Jeremiah delivers this promise from God, the children of Israel have been in captivity for 70 years. The people do not know if God's plan for prosperity, a hope, and a future will come to pass in their generation, but they can rest assured that it will certainly come to pass in the generations to come.

Matthew Henry, in his commentary on this verse, says, "He will give them, not the expectations of their fears, nor the expectations of their fancies, but the expectations of their faith, the end which he has promised and which will turn for the best to them."

This interpretation, "not the expectation of their fancies, but the expectation of their faith," resonates with me. The most "prosperous" woman I know did not prosper in a material way, nor did she gain any position of prominence. And she did not realize fully the "expectations of her faith" until well into her retirement years.

Leah Davids lived and worked sacrificially, under extremely difficult circumstances, for many years in Haiti. I don't know whether she went there against her will. I do know many Christians who have been compelled by the Holy Spirit—against their personal desire—to live and work in other such modern–day Babylons. The circumstances of their calling bring to mind the words of an old song: "He doesn't compel you to go against your will, He just makes you willing to go."

We were in Haiti recently for a weekend of anniversary meetings. Leah had also been invited to participate in the celebration. During one of the meetings, a bright–looking, very handsome young man asked her to join him on the platform, and he sang to Leah a song that had been especially written for her. When he concluded, the audience burst into thunderous and prolonged applause because they knew the story behind the song.

As a young woman, Leah had gone to a small Haitian village to gather the children who were designated to live in the children's home she administered. While in the village, she saw a set of tiny, sickly, extremely emaciated infant twins (a boy and a girl). They were not on her list, but Leah said, "I will take these two as well." The village authorities protested, saying, "Don't bother with them because they will not live much longer. They are not worth the trouble." But Leah insisted, and under her loving, patient care, the two children miraculously survived. The boy grew and developed into a very talented musician and composer. "Thank You For My Life" was the title of the song he dedicated to Leah on that memorable day. The prosperity that came to both of them cannot be measured in human terms. God didn't honor the expectation of their fancies; He honored the expectation of their faith.

Seek and Pray

Babylon is not confined to Haiti and other "third–

world" countries. There is a bit of Babylon in every city across America, as you will discover in a later section of this manual. Jeremiah's prophecy is relevant for this generation and for this unique time in our history. God is admonishing His people, today, to "seek and pray." The word *seek,* in this context, suggests, "working toward" the peace and prosperity of the cities. The Lord is saying to a 21st–century America, "If you work toward peace and prosperity for future generations, especially those struggling in the shadows of your cities, I will honor the expectations of your faith."

Essentials of Flight

Now let me get back to the flight plan analogy. Flight requires lift. He wants to give your life lift, but it is a gift that requires something from you. Wings are worthless without the flap (the work, the service). With God's ever–present lift and your corresponding committed service, there are no limits to how high you can soar. Why are some of God's people seemingly ineffective, living lives that appear dim and even hopeless? Why does the joy seem to be always dissipating in the lives of some Christians? Why are some saints so unhappy all the time? Why is His prosperity elusive to so many? Maybe it's because they want the lift without the flap, or the pull. They want the worship without the service, or the sacrifice. Worship gives lift. Service is the pull. The synchronization of these two elements is essential to flight.

If we are to be God's angels in this world and help fulfill his plans, we must have metaphorical wings, like the angels in the Bible. That book is filled with a host of images that I suspect have fed artists' imaginations in their portrayal of angels. I happen to think that the power of the Bible's figurative language can be applied to those of us who represent His army of earth angels. Isaiah uses such an image very effectively when he writes…

But those who wait on the Lord shall renew their strength; they shall mount up with wings like eagles…
—Isaiah 40:31a (NKJV)

God gives us metaphorical wings so that we might soar above the morass of this world with a strength and singleness of purpose that is other–wise and other–worldly. We are able to rise above the madding crowd and provide refuge to those who are hurting and crying out for help. David echoes this cry in one of his psalms and finds solace under the Lord's wings.

Be merciful to me, O God, be merciful to me! For my soul trusts in You; and in the shadow of Your wings I will make my refuge, until these calamities have passed by.
—Psalm 57:1 (NKJV)

Let me paraphrase another of the psalmist's prayers, as it should be prayed today.

Our Lord, you will always rule,
 but nations will vanish from the earth.
We are sent by You to listen to the longings of
 those who suffer and offer them hope.
And we will pay attention to their cries
 for help.

*And defend orphans (the fatherless) and
everyone else in need.*
—Psalm 10:16–18a

As I said earlier, this manual is about a revolutionary flight plan, one that will honor the expectation of our faith and take us to new heights—morally, ethically, and spiritually. This flight plan is about you and one of the most important decisions you will ever make.

Hope Is an Angel

Do angels exist? What role do they play in protecting our children? How dependent are they (both the angels and the children) upon the Christian community, His disciples (that's you and me)?

In Hebrews 1:14 (KJV), Paul describes angels as "ministering spirits, sent forth to minister for them who shall be heirs of salvation." Psalm 34:7 declares that "the angel of the Lord encampeth around about them that fear him, and delivereth them." Psalm 91:11 amplifies this truth as it says,

"For he shall give his angels charge over thee, to keep thee in all thy ways." Matthew 18:10 speaks of the ministry of angels to God's children and our responsibility, saying, "Take heed that ye despise not one of these little ones; for I say to you, that in heaven their angels do always behold the face of my Father which is in heaven." Hebrews 13:2 reminds us, "Do not forget to entertain strangers, for by so doing some have unwittingly entertained angels."

Children in their preadolescent, formative years have not yet reached the "age of accountability." I'm suggesting that these children can be placed in the "saints" category. They are heirs of salvation. If they should die before reaching the "age of accountability," they will automatically go to heaven. This is what the Scripture teaches: "for of such is the kingdom of heaven" (Matthew 19:14, KJV).

God has given his angels charge over the children. What is our responsibility as Christians toward them? We are not to despise these little ones. We have a God–given responsibility to protect them.

Maybe we should view ourselves as "angels in training," in an "angel apprenticeship program," "earth angels," or "angels incarnate." In this sense, the church embodies an "army of angels."

HOPE IS AN ANGEL. Jesus wanted His disciples then and he wants His disciples now to JOIN THE FLIGHT … for our future. He wants you to join the flight and claim His promises for you and for our children. He wants to prosper and honor the future through you. His plans include a "hope and a future" for those within your circle of influence, especially children.

Call to Flight!

Do angels exist? You bet they do! Not only must we believe in angels, but we are also encouraged to support them in their cause. Why should we be joining the flight with them? Because the future depends upon it.

I believe the following prophetic utterance to Isaiah was also meant as a prophetic call to the 21st–century church.

You shall raise up the foundations of many generations; you shall be called the repairer of the breach, the restorer of streets to live in. (Isaiah 58:12, KJV)

The book of Isaiah is like a miniature Bible. The first 39 chapters (like the 39 books of the Old Testament) are filled with blight, plight, and judgment. The final 27 chapters (like the 27 chapters of the New Testament) declare a message of hope and prosperity. As you read on you will find that this manual has a similar structural divergence.

In Isaiah 53 we find listed specific prophecies of Christ's atonement; among them is this key prophetic verse:

All we like sheep have gone astray; we have turned everyone, to his own way; and the Lord has laid on Him the iniquity of us all. (v.6)

The first two–thirds of this verse speaks to humankind's blight, plight, and judgment. The final third speaks of humankind's hope. Our *iniquity* (blight) was laid on Him. He became the atoning sacrifice so that our plight cycle might be broken. Nelson's *Illustrated Bible Dictionary* defines atonement this way: "The word can be broken into three parts which express this great truth in simple but profound terms: 'at–one–ment.' Through God's atoning grace and forgiveness, we are reinstated to a relationship of at–one–ment with God, in spite of our sin. We are at one with Him."

Portrait of Hope

Beginning with Isaiah 58, we see painted a prophetic picture of Israel's glorious future. It is a portrait of hope. The Messiah is coming to redeem His people. The prophecy has been fulfilled. We have witnessed this fulfillment through Scripture. How fortunate we are now to be living in the dispensation of hope. We who have been redeemed are His angels of hope, and we are called to paint a prophetic picture of America's glorious future. Hope is us! We are called to be repairers of the breach, the restorers of streets to live in.

Wingspread

Spreading your wings is essential to flight, and there is some risk when you first try it. You must learn and master some tricky aerodynamics. You may experience a few shaky landings (maybe a crash landing or two) along the way. And you may encounter some of those air pockets and storm clouds that are always lurking on the horizon. But taking off from your comfort zone and taking the risk will be worth it.

For this flight plan to succeed, many of you will need to spread your wings, metaphorically speaking. In fact, what the flight plan calls for is a massive flock of angels. With their wings outspread, they can, I believe, eventually cover the length and breadth of America and move beyond these shores until the whole earth is comforted in their shadow. God wants His people to "mount up with wings as eagles." He wants to span the globe with His love and compassion. God is in the control tower. The flight plan has been filed. And some angels have already spread their wings and taken flight.

Let us be inspired by them. And let us be inspired by the children who have found shelter in the shadow of those wings.

The Rest of the Story

We return to that critical juncture in Robert's life. Robert came home one day dressed in baggy gang clothing. His father was so infuriated that he ripped the clothes off his son's back and beat him severely. And when his mother attempted to intervene, she too was badly beaten.

Following the beating, Robert was forced to kneel, dressed only in his underwear, on the hot summer cement in his backyard. His father made him hold a brick over his head until he was told he could drop it. As Robert's body trembled, he was berated and told how useless and worthless he was. Robert was reminded again, as he had been so many times before, that he would never amount to anything.

"As my arms grew numb with pain," says Robert, "I wanted to throw the brick down and scream at him, 'You're a bad man! You're wrong! I am going to be something! I'm going to be a doctor some day and I'm going to help people!' "

It was during this same summer that Robert had encountered a living, caring earth angel—at a community swimming pool, of all places. Through a series of circumstances, a nearby church contracted to operate the pool through the summer months. With a membership of 400, this was not a mega–church by Orange County standards. It was a church, however, made up primarily of professional people who felt a compelling compassion to reach the children living in the pockets of poverty right in their own backyards.

Doug was a member of this church and director of the swimming program. Eavesdrop for a moment on the encounter that occurred between Robert and Doug.

"Whoa! Slow down. No running."

"Sorry."

"That's O.K., buddy. I just don't want you to slip and hurt yourself, that's all. You wouldn't want to wind up in the hospital would you?"

"I like hospitals. I'm going to be a doctor someday."

"Is that right? How would you like to learn first aid? We have a boys' program at our church where you can learn first aid and a lot of other fun things."

"First aid" was the magical phrase that commanded Robert's attention. Doug's angel antenna had extended intuitively. The connection was made and the invitation given. Doug took a special interest in Robert, who soon found himself totally involved in Sunday School and the music programs of the church. This was a critical phase in the formation of Robert's spiritual, moral, and ethical foundation.

Robert's teenage years came and, along with them, inevitable peer pressure. He drifted back into old habits. He connected with the wrong crowd again. In a nasty fight, his nose was shattered, and he needed plastic surgery. The first doctor was impatient with Robert's curiosity about medicine. So he and his mother sought out another surgeon.

Dr. Robert Beltran explained the various medical instruments as he used them on Robert, and he even let Robert put the stethoscope on and listen to his own heartbeat. The doctor's attention, along with the fact that he, like Robert, was of Mexican heritage, made a deep impression on the young man, and he confided to Dr. Beltran that he, too, wanted to be a surgeon one day.

The surgery was successfully completed, but Dr. Beltran didn't stop seeing Robert. His angel antenna extended, and he took Robert under his wing. During the summer months, Robert performed odd jobs around the medical center and was even allowed to watch the doctor perform surgery on occasion. He encouraged Robert to take his studies seriously and "not lose the dream." In high school, Robert became captain of the football team and senior class president, and he went on to become a proud graduate of UCLA.

The good doctor is still his mentor. When Robert first visited Dr. Beltran, he was just beginning to practice medicine. Today Dr. Beltran is one of the leading ENT specialists/plastic surgeons in Orange

County and a board member at University of California, Irvine (UCI) Medical School. Doug's ministry was also in its incubational stage when he first encountered Robert. He felt the call to ministry, went on to become fully ordained, and is now successfully engaged in his chosen vocation.

Robert is also reaping the bounty of God's promises. His faith remains strong, and he was recently accepted into medical school at UCI, on a full scholarship. He will quickly tell you that this would not have been possible without the intervention of some "earth angels" who perceptively reached out to him in a loving and caring way. They (Doug, Dr. Beltran, and Robert) responded to God's plan for a "hope and a future," and it is now being prophetically realized. God continues to honor the expectation of their faith.

ANGELS ALL AROUND

Garage Gathering

Vi Brown and her husband, Jerry, live in Mission Viejo, California, an affluent suburb. Together, they own and operate a thriving insurance business. Twenty–five years ago, when their two children were young, Vi was led to begin a Sunday School in her garage. She was concerned not only about her own children, but also about the neighbor children, boys and girls who would inevitably influence each other as they grew into adolescence. She was all too familiar with the pitfalls and pressures facing this emerging generation, and she wanted to do her part in shaping their future.

She went door to door, passing out flyers and talking to parents about her concerns and desires. Her message resonated with many, and soon parents were not only sending their children but also volunteering to assist Vi in her noble adventure. Because Vi elected to spread her wings and join the flight, the future of that neighborhood has taken on a kind of "halo" effect. We may never know the true magnitude of that effect until we reach the other side of Glory.

Vi's children are grown now and successfully pursuing professional careers. And Vi, after 25 years, still sacrificially and faithfully gathers the neighborhood children in her garage. God continues to honor the expectation of her faith.

Family Extraordinaire

In 2002, my wife, Doris, and I had one of those rare and serendipitous encounters with an extraordinary couple, Bob and Dorothy DeBolt. We were seated next to them at a dinner celebrating the opening of the Ray and Joan Kroc Community Center in San Diego. I quickly learned that they were the parents of 20 children. We were blown away when we learned about the special circumstances of these children and the astonishing love and commitment of the whole family.

Nine of the kids were physically challenged—blind, paralyzed, abandoned, and abused. The adopted children include seven from Vietnam; four from Korea; one from Mexico; and two Americans, one white and one black. One child is a congenital quadruple amputee who was classified as unadoptable.

Dorothy credits her own spiritual formation as her foundation for the strength and stamina needed for this extraordinary challenge. Sunday School played an important and critical role in her own children's upbringing and development. In her own words…

> *Sunday School was a constant for me as a child. I was taught that being a real Christian meant helping others. And my parents also set this example for me. When [Dorothy's and Bob's] family was starting, we joined an interdenominational community church in the San Francisco Bay Area. The older children joined me in teaching Sunday School there. One of our favorite activities became the church–sponsored Summer Camp called "Lode Star" in the*

foothills of Northern California. It was an annual interracial camp specifically set up for poor children from the Bay cities area—children who had never before experienced camping. All this made a large impact on the hearts and minds of my growing family.

After we began adopting so many physically challenged children, we continued our church membership. However, due to the encumbrances and difficulties of handling crutches, braces, and wheelchairs, we held Sunday School sessions at home. Many of our grandchildren now share in their own Sunday School experiences.

This amazing family adapted itself to God's plan for them—"plans for a hope and a future." Dorothy reports, "All twenty of our adult children are now fiercely, proudly independent. All are imbued with a true sense of self–worth. They are now instilling those same values in our thirty grandchildren and one great–grandchild." God continues to honor the expectation of this family's faith. For more information on the DeBolt family, go to www.debolts.com.

Beam of Light

Robert Muzikowski, his wife, and six children moved into Chicago's West Side because, in his words, "We felt we couldn't reach out to the community without being a part of it, so we moved our family [here] to be a beam of light in the neighborhood."

Muzikowski's story is proof positive that God's "plans for prosperity, a hope and a future," are not just empty promises. Addiction to drugs and alcohol had plagued Bob's early life. Through a divinely inspired set of circumstances, he pulled his life together and eventually created Chicago's largest Little League baseball program, which is now spreading nationwide. It's Little League with a plus, as he explains in an interview with "Zondervan Pathways."

> *AA taught me I could live a sober life one day at a time; so I figured anyone could*

clean up an abandoned field one broken bottle or one crushed can at a time. My faith and the examples I'd witnessed had taught me that being a Christian means truly believing what Jesus said about loving my neighbor, the Golden Rule, and honoring him by serving all my neighbors—not just the ones who could serve me back.

We had determined from the beginning that there would be another difference. We would make it crystal clear to everyone at the outset that this was a faith–based program. We began all our meetings, programs, and games with prayer. Almost everyone understood it was faith that motivated the start of the league and that it was our faith that kept us coming back.

Each team became a caring Christian community. The teams' activities extended beyond the baseball field and were designed to strengthen the social, spiritual, and emotional well–being of every child involved. The coach's homes became safe havens, giving respite and refuge when needed. Some coaches began to provide scholarships for players; a few even became foster parents to some of the children. The coaches' obsession was not with winning a game, but rather with teaching these boys and girls how to win in life.

And I like the advice Bob gives to those thinking about volunteering: "Stop sitting out the war … there's something going on in every community. You can get involved wherever you are." He adds, "Everybody looks at problems like drugs and gangs, and throws their hands up. If they just did a few little things, it would be amazing what they could accomplish. We're supposed to love our neighbor as ourselves, and that's what helps build a community." God continues to honor the expectation of his faith. Robert Muzikowski can be reached at muz@connect5.com if you would like more information on how to get involved.

No Respecter of Persons

We can't help but rejoice in these successes, but we should not forget that many children still live in the ugly glare of abuse, neglect, and poverty. Let us also remember that abuse and neglect is no respecter of persons. There is poverty of spirit abiding in the middle and upper echelons of our society as well. Abuse insidiously permeates the infrastructure of middle–class and even upper–class America. Neglect rears its ugly head in the Nob Hills and Newports, and it is emblematic of the changing morality that is overtaking this nation. The escalating divorce rate is but one symptom of this malaise. Unfortunately, it is the children who suffer most. For those children, a sheltering shadow is conspicuous by its absence. Let us be motivated by that missing shadow of comfort and hope.

But be forewarned. The present picture is not pretty, and your prescribed involvement will be daunting. Be prepared to take off from your comfort zone. This flight, should you decide to take it, will wing you into enemy territory, where danger lurks, enemies abound, and intrigue entangles.

Do you want to graduate from angel "wannabe" to bonafide earth angel? I want to help you in this process, but I also warn you that you should proceed with caution. Before you make that decision to don your wings, you must understand what you are up against, and you must consider the risks involved.

HELL!
The Blight Path

The flight path of history is strewn with the wreckage of a blighted humanity. You might call it the "blight path." This path, paved with decadence, is so attractive that millions are clamoring to travel it. It is the path that leads to destruction, to hell.

I suggest you travel another path. But I must warn you that this way is not fashionable or trendy; traveling it will require sacrifice, self–denial, and an uncomfortable vulnerability. It is a path of giving and forgiving, where getting is secondary and greed is non–existent. On this path, pleasure is not a temporal, momentary "feel–good" thing, but an eternal, permanent "real–good" thing. Oh, there is a present pleasure to be sure, but it comes with a price. The kind of promised satisfaction I propose will take some getting used to, and the process will stretch you immeasurably.

Read on at your own risk. Your life may be changed forever.

The Blight Knight

Satan is the sinister force we are up against. Make no mistake: His existence is literal and his presence is formidable. The father of blight, he has prepared his own customized flight plan for us. Jesus refers to him as the prince of this world (John 14:30) and the father of lies (John 8:44). His legendary legions are a real, present force to be reckoned with. They are angels of the surreal kind, and they have always existed. In his fall from God's favor, Satan persuaded one third of the angels to join him in his rebellion (Rev. 12:3–4).

Look around. You will see their handiwork everywhere. As you did with those computerized posters that were so popular a couple of years back, you'll have to refocus your eyes to see the "hidden picture." Satan is the master of disguises, and his legions are experts at camouflaging what is really going on. That which is deadly appears attractive. Ugliness is veiled in beauty. Pain is cloaked in pleasure. Satan twists the truth and uses chicanery to confuse us about what is real. Deception melded with trickery is a part of his *modus operandi.* Illusion is his secret weapon.

Let me illustrate.

No Smoking

The tobacco industry, under Satan's spell, has perfected the art of illusion. Cigarette sellers are masters at pushing the pleasure while masking the pain. Let me tell you about some of the pain. I watched my mother die a slow, agonizing death. Her younger sister suffered severely with smoke–induced emphysema. When these women were young in the 30s, the media romanticized smoking as the fashionable thing to do. But the end for my mother and her sister was neither romantic nor fashionable.

My brother died from smoking–related cancer at 47. During his vulnerable teen years, he had been targeted by the tobacco industry. The Marlboro Man captured his fancy, and that of an entire generation. Tobacco, a mass serial killer still legitimized by advertising, has been loosed on another naive emerging generation, one of my own sons included.

In the mid–80s, studies showed that children under 6 recognized Joe Camel more readily than they did Mickey Mouse. More recently, the tobacco industry has been indicted for campaigns specifically targeted at young people and designed to lure a new generation of smokers.

Talk about deception, trickery, and chicanery. And yet, our taxes support subsidies to the tobacco industry. Cancer research organizations accept tobacco industry financial support, even though tobacco use has been established as the primary cause of lung cancer and has been associated with many other types of cancer, as well as with heart disease and a legion of other ills. Tobacco kills more Americans each year than alcohol, cocaine, crack, heroin, homicide, suicide, car accidents, fires, and AIDS combined.

Make no mistake about it: The Father of Lies continues to strut his stuff. Be wary. Your son or daughter might be the next casualty.

And John Stossel reported in his "Give Me A Break" segment on the ABC program 20/20 that

Phillip Morris is spending $150 million a year on advertising designed to puff (pun intended) their charitable giving, which amounts to $115 million a year. Why not give the total $265 million to charity? Because this would not help them create the new charitable image they are trying to achieve while going on with business as usual. "Give me a break!" says John Stossel. This ad campaign features the master illusionist at work.

In–Flight Entertainment

Refocus your eyes once more and see what is going on behind the glitz in the entertainment industry. Sex and violence are big business at the box office. The bigger–than–life screen magically makes the deadly appear attractive. And the small screen often paints colorful pictures of decadence.

A feature in *Time* magazine (Nov. 27, 2000) was headlined, "It's here, it's QUEER, get used to it." The subhead reads, "A daring series about gays burns down the closet." The article describes the show: "…mostly it's about sex. The adrenaline–

charged opening begins in a pheromone–drenched disco on Pittsburgh's gay Mecca, Liberty Avenue, then hurtles at 200 beats a minute into an outré lust scene between 29–year–old rake Brian (Gale Harold) and Justin (Randy Harrison), a kid of 17—count 'em, 17—years. No conveniently arranged sheets, no angst, no kisses shot from the back: in 10 minutes, QAF opens the closet of gay TV sexuality and chucks in a neon stick of dynamite." Believe it or not, this is describing an actual scene from a successful TV series, "Queer as Folk," on "Showtime." And the rest of the industry is now scrambling to "catch up."

In the entertainment world, promiscuity is aggrandized; in the real world, the AIDS virus kills. In the entertainment world, violence is glorified; in the real world, drive–by shootings kill. In the entertainment world, the drug culture is hyped; in the real world, speed kills. The prince of this world knows his way around tinsel town; he uses the silver screen to confuse and confound the truth.

And who are the victims? Our children. Satan

attacks them in their innocence, when they have trouble separating reality and fantasy. He hits them when they are most malleable and where they are most vulnerable. The choices children make during these formative years will play themselves out into adulthood. Do you know what your child is watching tonight?

A World of Paradoxes

Do I believe in free speech? Yes! Do I want censorship? Absolutely! I know what you're thinking. "Sounds to me like this writer doesn't know whether he's coming or going!" Wait a minute! Follow my reasoning.

True, my two statements create a paradox. But I have news for you. We are living in a world of paradoxes. Satan is the patron saint of paradoxes. David Myers in *The American Paradox,* asks this question, "Are we better off than we were 40 years ago?" this way:

> *Materially yes, morally no. Therein lies the American paradox. We now have, as average*

Americans, doubled real incomes and doubled what money buys. We have espresso coffee, the World Wide Web, sport utility vehicles, and caller ID. And we have less happiness, more depression, more fragile relationships, less communal commitment, less vocational security, more crime, and more demoralized children.

Is there a little bit of Babylon in America?

It is the demoralized state of our children that disturbs me. Free speech is for those whose psyches are fully formed. Censorship is absolutely essential during a child's formative years. Marion Wright Edelman of the Children's Defense Fund says, "All our children are growing up today in an ethically polluted nation where instant sex without responsibility, instant gratification without effort, instant solutions without sacrifice, getting rather than giving, and hoarding rather than sharing are the too–frequent signals of our mass media." Notice that Edelman says, "all our children," not just the children of poverty.

In a chapter titled, "Media, Minds, and the Public Good," David Myers gives ample evidence to support this statement. Let me share a few excerpts to pique your curiosity and whet your appetite:

All told, television beams its electromagnetic waves into children's eyeballs for more growing–up hours than they spend in school. More hours, in fact, than they spend in any other waking activity. From these hours— 20,000 hours diverted from talking, playing, reading, and so forth—what do children learn? (p. 200)

With most children now arriving at an empty home after school, does late–afternoon television fare matter? Does it matter if, instead of leaving our children to Beaver, we leave them to Beavis? Does viewing prime–time crime influence their thinking and acting? Does on–screen sex shape their sexual perceptions, expectations, and behavior? Do the media mold us? Mirror us? Or both? (p. 196)

Free speech and censorship—can they live in harmony together? I think they must—for the sake of our children and our future.

Listen to me! Satan and his minions are alive and well on this planet. And don't kid yourself; they're not paying that much attention to you. You've already decided which path to take. No, the negative creative energy of Satan's legions is concentrated on our children. Satan's minions know what will influence the future. They reason, "Get the children during their formative years and we will have them for life. Get them on the blight path early, and chances are they will never stray from it. Blight their psyches early, and odds are they will pass the plague on from generation to generation. Blight is might!"

Gravitational Pull

The blight path is Satan's domain. As a powerful gravitational force, his pull is always downward.

To jump out of an airplane and free fall must be an exhilarating feeling, and if I were not such a coward, I would love to try it. But this exhilaration, when it comes to our moral choices, is another of Satan's illusions—using the thrill of the moment to distract us from future consequences. While we may enjoy the experience now, we are headed for a crash landing. The fact is, most of the world is in free fall, without wings or a parachute.

We don't want to participate in the free fall. We want to participate in the "free for all," the grace of God that is free for all and "lifts us out of the miry clay." It is the gift and lift of His grace that keeps us from falling. But I'm getting ahead of myself. So let me bring you back down to earth—all the way down.

Hell's Bells

Let me take you into the abyss of Satan's domain. He is the quintessential serial killer, a supernatural mafioso of the transcendental kind. The horror of his handiwork is without peer or measure. He has been loosed with free reign in our universe.

We sing, "Ring the bells of heaven, there is joy today for a soul returning from the wild! Glory, glory how the angels sing!" I suspect that heaven doesn't have a corner on the bell or angelic choir market. I wouldn't be surprised if hell's bells ring and hell's angels sing every time a soul refuses to leave the wild. I'll bet the sound is ear–splitting when a saint succumbs to the satanic gravitational pull. I'm sure the gleeful choir is discordant and deafening when a child is born addicted to crack or is sexually abused and/or emotionally neglected.

Hell's bells ring with great consistency, clarity, and alacrity. There is never a dull moment in the bell tower. And the reverberations resonate with great power here on earth. The colloquialism often used to describe this phenomenon is "hell on earth." Jesus pointed to a specific earthly place, Gehenna, as a way to understand what the place of eternal punishment is like. Listen to this description from Nelson's *Illustrated Bible Dictionary.*

Hell as a place of punishment translates Gehenna, the Greek form of the Hebrew word that means 'the vale of Hinnom'— a valley just south of Jerusalem. In this valley the Canaanites worshiped Baal and the fire god Molech by sacrificing their children in a fire that burned continuously. Even Ahaz and Manasseh, kings of Judah, were guilty of this terrible, idolatrous practice (2 Chr. 28:3; 33:6).

In the time of Jesus the Valley of Hinnom was used as the garbage dump of Jerusalem. Into it were thrown all the filth and garbage of the city, including the dead bodies of animals and executed criminals. To consume all this, fires burned constantly. Maggots worked in the filth. When the wind blew from that direction over the city, its awfulness was quite evident. At night, wild dogs howled and gnashed their teeth as they fought over the garbage.

Jesus used this awful scene as a symbol of hell. In effect he said, 'Do you want to know what hell is like? Look at the valley of Gehenna.' So hell may be described as God's 'cosmic garbage dump.' All that is unfit for heaven will be thrown into hell.

Hellish spots like this one abound in every generation and on every continent. Do you want to know what hell is like? Take a trip to the Holocaust Museum in Washington, D.C., and you will get a glimpse. Travel with a television news commentator to Serbia, Rwanda, or a thousand other places on this planet and you will sniff the fragrance. Walk with me (as I did Sept. 12, 2001) into the smoking carnage at Ground Zero, where the World Trade Center Towers once stood, and you will feel the pull of its gravity. I've been to the garbage dump in Manila, in the Philippines, where a whole colony of human beings grovel day and night for their livelihood. This is their home—the place they eat, sleep, recreate, defecate and procreate. A garbage dump is their world. I have traveled with the Discovery

Channel into the sewers of Calcutta and Rio de Janeiro, where millions of children coexist with slime–infested rats. Stink–filled sewers are their world.

Come with me into the ghettos of the most affluent country that has ever existed on the face of this planet, our America, and you will taste another sample of hell on earth. You don't have to travel far from your doorstep to find an abused or neglected child, one that is living in a literal garbage dump. Sound far–fetched? Trust me, I've been there—in Honolulu, San Francisco, Los Angeles, Phoenix, Dallas, Chicago, Cleveland, Philadelphia, New York City and, yes, even Flagstaff, Arizona. I can take you to any city in America and show you one of those cosmic dumps. I have sat on garbage–littered couches in homes where the stench is unbearable. I have seen maggots crawling out of rotting garbage. I have peeked into homes where cupboards are bare; such pantries are not found just in nursery rhymes. I've been to Hollywood Boulevard, where all is not glitter and gold. Instead, the street teems with child prostitutes, runaways, abandoned boys and girls trying to survive as best they can under living conditions that are indescribable. I've ventured into crack houses that define the "Vale of Hinnom."

What I am describing is real. These conditions are not an aberration or anomaly. They exist in abundance and the stench is worsening. Hell's bells are ringing with greater frequency. Is there a little bit of Babylon in America?

Again I ask, who are the victims? I find it interesting that the Canaanites worshiped their Gods by sacrificing children. We view such an act with abhorrence. But I wonder, are we doing the same thing today? Are we guilty of sacrificing our children in the "Gehenna holes" of America? And these holes are not confined to the ghettos. They can also be found in the fatherless, motherless, loveless, after–school–empty homes scattered throughout suburbia. The children are not sacrificing themselves, are they? We can't place all the blame on their parents, can we? Aren't those parents also victims of their circumstances, of successive generations, of a world that we have helped create? May I be so bold to suggest that the lion's share of the blame and shame must fall to us, we who have turned a deaf ear and a blind eye, we who have committed the sin of omission? Make no mistake: Our hands are tightly wound around the rope in the bell tower. We must bear some responsibility for the blight on this nation and for the plight of our children.

Fasten Your Seatbelts

I cautioned you that the ride would not be a smooth one. Bumps and air pockets are to be expected, so the seatbelt sign is on. I warned you to be prepared to leave your comfort zone. Prepare to become increasingly more uncomfortable as you refocus your eyes to see the blight and unstop your ears to hear the cries for help.

HELP!
THE PLIGHT PATTERN

Blight is a blemish, an affliction that leads to deterioration and, ultimately, to destruction. Our plight, then, is the pattern of consequences that emerge from a blighted condition. The very first blight occurred in the Garden of Eden, where Satan disguised himself as a serpent and performed his first master illusion. A genesis moment for humanity came when Adam and Eve bit into God's forbidden fruit because they wanted to believe Satan's lie. Their act is referred to theologically as "original sin." That original blight upon humanity has been passed on from generation to generation with unending repercussions and deadly consequences. I refer to this process as "the plight pattern."

This continuing consequential pattern first manifested itself in the life of Cain, who slew his brother Abel. What had begun with Cain's and Abel's parents, two unsuspecting but culpable individuals, took root in their children and their children's children; today, there are 6 billion people living on this planet who have inherited these patterns. As you can see, the mathematical implications are infinitesimal.

Sometimes, God has become so angry with human sin and disobedience that he has intervened through famine, flood, and pestilence. But mostly, He has forgiven His people time and again, and counted on them to follow Him in helping to break the powerful pattern of sin and death. Throughout history, God's chosen people, His followers, have also been God's intervening agents. When the emphasis has been on "seek and pray," they have prospered. And therein lies the premise of this book. But before we delve into this I want to explore some present–day plight patterns, and the cries for help that rise from them. Our understanding of these things, I believe, is critical to the future.

The Patterns of Poverty

> *They shout, but nobody hears them. They sleep outside, yet nobody sees them. And they ask for opportunities, but nobody answers their prayers. They are called the poor.*
> —*Rey Ramsey* (horizonMag.com)

The statistics are staggering. To have food on your table three times a day, let alone once or twice, is the exception, not the norm in our world. As a result, malnutrition is a disease of epidemic proportions.

More than 6 million children die of malnutrition each year, according to the UNICEF report, "The State of the World's Children, 1998." At present, 3 billion people worldwide live on less than $2 per day, while 1.3 billion get by on less than $1 per day.

Mountains to the Valleys

What about America, the land of plenty and promise? Has this poverty pattern invaded the land of the free and the home of the brave? Is God really blessing all of America "from the mountains to the valleys to the oceans white with foam?" Can we really sing with comfort and conviction and confidence that America is "home sweet home" to every child? Do those romantic "amber waves of grain" fill their small stomachs? Now is the hour to get our proverbial heads out of the sand. America, it is time to open your eyes and unplug your ears! The stark reality, if we choose to pay attention, is frightening. The Child Poverty Fact Sheet (June 2001) compiled by the National Center for Children in Poverty should give us all pause for thought. Let us face the truth head on without excuse—and with apology. The report states: "America's children are more likely to live in poverty than Americans in any other age group. Despite significant improvements since 1993, there are more children in poverty today than there were two decades ago."

And listen to this! The report goes on to state, "The United States' child poverty rate is substantially higher—often two to three times higher—than that of most other major Western industrialized nations." Nearly 20% of our youngest children live in poverty, and they are often subject to abuse and neglect. I refer to them as the invisible 20%, and in my opinion, it is these children to whom the church must begin to pay more attention.

There is so much to digest in all of the statistics and reports available, but it is the relentless cycles or patterns that must concern us. What happens during these early years is critical to the future. And prevention has historically been low on the priority scale.

Other Plight Patterns

Poverty is the breeding ground for the proliferation of more severe plight patterns. Listen to the message contained in these revealing statistics from *The American Paradox.*

"Since 1976, when data were first gathered from all 50 states, the number of children reported neglected and abused has nearly quintupled, to 3.2 million a year." (p. 63)

"In 1960, 15 percent of births to 15– to 19–year–olds were outside of marriage. In 1997,

78 percent were." (p. 14)

"A U.S. government study in 1996 found that children of single parents are 80 percent more at risk for abuse or neglect." (p. 63)

We are becoming a fatherless society, and it's spreading like a cancer throughout the world. The result is that child abuse is skyrocketing. Illegitimacy and abuse (substance, sexual, and physical) are closely connected. Illegitimacy, poverty, and abuse are linked together and feed off one another.

And what are some of the consequences? Myers includes in his book this prophetic letter to the President of the United States of America. (p. 98)

Dear Mr. Clinton,

I want you to stop the killing in the city. People is dead and I think that somebody might kill me. So would you please stop the people from deading. I'm asking you nicely to stop it. I know you can do it. Do it. I now you could. Your friend James.

James Darby, 9, from New Orleans, wrote this letter on April 29, 1994. On May 8, little more than a week later, James was killed in a drive–by shooting.

According to Myers, the "American paradox" is this: "We are a nation of historically unparalleled wealth, affluence and influence and conversely poverty, illegitimacy, abuse and the resulting pathology is skyrocketing in unequaled proportions."

Open your eyes, America! Wake up, clergy! Hear this 21st–century prophetic utterance! The emerging patterns are clear, and the time has come to do something about it.

We sing, "God Bless America"—and He has done that, beyond what our forefathers ever dreamed or imagined. With increased blessing comes increased responsibility. Ignore the responsibility, and there are sure to be consequences. If we allow the present patterns to continue, I believe God will hold us accountable. Jesus illustrated this for us when He told the story of a beggar named Lazarus who lay outside the door of a rich man's home. He died hungry, diseased, and hopeless. The rich man also died and his soul went into hell. In torment he saw Lazarus in the far distance comforted in the bosom of Abraham. The rich man was held accountable because he was hard hearted in spite of his great blessings (Luke 16:19–30).

Penetrating a Barrier

The 9/11 attack on America was horrific, the death and carnage reprehensible. The whole world watched as those jets slammed into the World Trade Center. It took place right before our very eyes. The attacks have penetrated a barrier of emotional immunity. We are still a nation in mourning, a nation together committed to eliminating the root cause of this evil. This is a noble endeavor.

At the very same time, the National Clearinghouse on Child Abuse and Neglect Information reports an estimated 2,000 annual deaths resulting from abuse and neglect in America. Experts such as Ryan Rainey from the National Center for Prosecution of Child Abuse believe that the number of child deaths per year from maltreatment may be as high as 5,000.

There's an old saying that "what the eye cannot see the heart cannot grieve."

These attacks on our children are just as horrific and reprehensible as the World Trade Center attacks. Those assaults took place before our very eyes; the assaults on our children, by and large, do not. This is an invisible carnage eating away at the heart of America. The nation is not mourning the loss of these children. We are not united and committed to eliminating the root cause of this evil. The plight of children has not penetrated the barrier of our emotional immunity. Yet the cause is just as noble as the pursuit of the terrorists who attacked our nation.

The death of the children alone ought to make us madder than hell! What about the neglected and abused children who do not die but live with the hell of their memories? What kind of pain and carnage will they inflict on future generations? What does the knowledge of this plight demand from us?

Relaxed moral attitudes have, in my estimation, contributed to a proliferation of more severe plight patterns. And they, unfortunately, permeate every echelon of society. And it's the children whose psyches are damaged most. Think about it. Myers writes, "Since 1960, the divorce rate has doubled, the teen suicide rate has tripled, the percentage of babies born to unmarried parents has (excuse the pun) sextupled, cohabitation (a predictor of future divorce) has increased sevenfold and depression has soared—to ten times the pre–World War II level, by one estimate." Make no mistake about it; middle–class America, and its children, are not immune to these debilitating plight patterns.

A Fresh Sense of Urgency

The plight of our children demands from us a fresh sense of urgency. I heard a medical missionary recount the following story. He was sent to a hospital in India. On the very first day they brought in a young woman who had a malignant growth on her neck. One look, and the doctor knew it was incurable. Several weeks later he was making his rounds and came upon this woman lying on her cot. She looked up with pleading eyes and asked the doctor for help. All he could say was, "I'm sorry, but you have come too late. If you had only come a year or two earlier, we could have helped you." She said, "No doctor, I'm not the one who is late. You are the one who is late. Two years ago, the hospital wasn't here and a year ago, you weren't here. You are the one who is late."

Let's not be the ones who are "late." This story gives me a fresh sense of urgency, a fresh understanding that we cannot ignore our children's cries for help.

Nor can we isolate ourselves from the world scene. Are we "better" because we are a nation blessed with wealth and power? The answer is an emphatic, "No!" Should our "blessed" status increase our humility and fuel our sense of responsibility? The answer is an emphatic, "Yes!" Should we share our resources? Absolutely! The world is shrinking because of technological advances. We can no longer insulate ourselves from the plight that plagues the more impoverished parts of this world. The penetrating AIDS virus, as just one example, ought to serve as a clarion wakeup call. America is not immune to it.

The World Health Organization has reported that "an estimated 5.3 million people, including 600,000 children under age 15, became infected with the virus that causes AIDS this year (2000). Worldwide, 36.1 million adults and children are estimated to be living with AIDS or the virus, split almost equally between men and women. In the two decades since the disease was recognized, it has killed an estimated 21.8 million people, including 3 million this year." (*The New York Times*, Nov. 25, 2000)

I recently made a trip to South Africa and Mozambique. It has been determined that 23% of the population in that region carries the AIDS virus—that's almost a ratio of 1 in 4. My fertile imagination raced and my pulse quickened with every fourth or fifth person I passed as I walked the teeming streets of Cape Town, Johannesburg,

Pretoria, Soweto, and Maputo. It was an overpowering and extremely sobering visualization.

The five senses were fully throttled as tension filled the air. You could see it. You could feel it. You could hear it. You could taste it. You could smell it!

Our hotel was filled with young people attending an AIDS prevention conference. The message emblazoned on their T–shirts screamed out, "You can make a difference!" Many wore red ribbons printed on their T–shirts and pinned to their clothing. The symbol was plastered everywhere imaginable. Billboards juxtaposed Yogi Berra's proclamation, "The future ain't what it used to be," with the AIDS protestation of "Help!"

There is a sense of urgency gripping South Africa. There is a sense of urgency gripping us all, and AIDS is but a symptom of something much deeper and more profound. Put your ear to the ground and listen to the mournful, plaintive cries for help—this time from our children, whether they are in South Africa or our own back yard.

I found the following cry for help pinned to a bulletin board in a children's home in South Africa. Figuratively, in our own nation, it should be pinned to the walls of all dysfunctional homes, displayed on the bulletin boards of a failed foster care system, scrawled on the doors of poorly managed child–care institutions and printed in the pages of our Sunday church bulletins.

I am from a children's home. I come from nowhere. I don't expect you to like me. I don't expect you to care. Because no one has before. But if you do, I don't trust you. My past is dark with shadows and pain. And now I'm in a children's home. I don't do well in school. I act out and get bad grades. I don't want to be expelled, but I'm from the children's home. All the kids are like me. They all act out. They smoke and they swear, and we all live together. We are the same because we all live in the children's home, although few of us tell our friends. Because where we live is who we are. We are the children's home. A place of troubles and hurts. A place with no hope. Because everyone who enters has a problem, is a problem. And I have no hope. I have no future. I have no choice. When I'm bad, I am excused. It's normal for me to misbehave. It's expected. I have no choice. I'm from a children's home.

So give me hope, give me freedom, give me education, give me support, give me comfort, give me a future. I won't find these things on my own. I am incapable because after all, I live in a children's home. And my future holds only problems. I am from a children's home. And when I'm thirty I will still live in a children's home, not in body, but in mind.
—*Anonymous*

HELP!

Listen to these prayers for help written in their own handwriting by two children in one of our inner–city church programs here in the United States.

Dear God,

I know that I have done some thing's that I know is rong. But I still turn around and do them anyways. God to me it seems like no one understands what I go through. God you know that my dad has been working hard but its still not enough to feed me, my sister, my brother, my mom, my dad, my 2 cousents that live with me. God I feel alone and God you know that my mom is on drug's and she doen't know but when she comes home in the middle of the night I pray that she will stay home, and just pray and thank God for what he has done. I cry my self to sleep at night just thinking about my family. God we don't have the money to put our phone on but you will make a way out of know way. A lot of things are going on in my life and I don't know what to do God help me I am traped in a little box that

I can't get out. I need you to help me God I don't know what to do. I am in a lot of stress. I need you to help me. I feel like killing my self. I am not good at nothing. I just need you in my life right now.

HELP!!!

Dear God,

I went to school, when teacher's would yell at me for no reason, most of the time I would yell back but every seence that Wednesday we prayed the devil has been working faster and harder to mess up my life. So far he has my mom. And know he trying to get me and my sister. God, I'm going to get right down to the point. To me its like your not there. I do what I know is right (sometimes). I am only human. I'm going to make mistake. I'm going to slip and fall I need is a strong person or friend to help me back up. God I wish you would send me some one older, much older then me that I can talk to and that I can pray with. If you will just help my mother I will be so so so so so so happy. Sometimes we go to bed with out eating but I know you will make a way. When I don't have clean clothes to ware I know you will make a way. God thank you giving me a piece of mind and giving me a family even if it looks like worst family ever. I know its not about gifts but if its ok can I get just one thing. All I want is my mother to be free from drugs/…God if you come back, can you send some one to help (me) to be ready. I will do what it takes…God just help me.

HELP!

Imitation of Life

Mine is the voiceless cry of every victimized child. Abuse, poverty, and neglect are no respecters of persons. I come in every shape, size, color, and culture. I am young, mal-

leable, and easily influenced. I have tremendous potential—for good or for bad.

The way I am shaped will shape the future, and I am shaped by what I see and experience. I will imitate life. How I will live as an adult will be conditioned by the preview of life I receive in my formative years. I will imitate life. If life around me is distorted, my view of life will be distorted. I will imitate life. If my perceptions are misguided, my actions will be also. I will imitate life.

The reality I comprehend is formulated by the unreality that penetrates my limited and cloistered world. My innocence is matched by my naiveté. I do not control my destiny. It is controlled by the handful of people around me, people who, like me, once represented the future, people who continue to imitate life as it was imitated for them.

I am looking for an angel. Only God's representative angel can help me pierce the darkness and find the true light. Only an angel can help me change this inherited ugliness into real beauty. Only an intervening angel can help me break the never-ending cycle of despair and make hope happen. I am looking for God's angel. Are you that angel?

HELP!

Are you listening with your heart? The pleas for help can be heard no other way. This world needs more angels—angels that come in your size, shape, and color —enough guardian angels to match every wanting child on the face of this darkening planet. Together we can make this a better world. Together we can we can dispel the darkness. Together we can light up the world. Together we can make hope happen.

HOPE!
THE FLIGHT PLAN
(Amplified)

We have come full circle. This flight manual began with hope and it will end with hope. Hope is not something that manifests itself out of thin air. People must have a reason to hope. It is our responsibility to "make hope happen," not only for ourselves, but also for our children and our children's children.

Clarion Call to Flight

How can we do this? Earlier on I issued a call to flight and now I want to make it a clarion call. I want you to close your eyes, hear the trumpets sound, and see the King of Kings coming in all His glory. I want you to feel the brilliance of His presence and touch the pierced palm of His outstretched hand. I want you to sense the majesty of that resurrection morning when you will be lifted up and literally fly into His presence. But I don't want you to wait until that day to experience His glory. I want you to "join the flight" today and enjoy the plans He has for you right now, "… plans to prosper you … plans to give you a hope and a future."

Before I get into the specifics of how to "make hope happen," let me share with you a litany of "what ifs?" Begin to "wonder" and personalize these stories as you "seek and pray" for divine guidance and direction.

WHAT IF?

Her Story

A recent article in *The New York Times* gives us a hint of what might happen when the shadow of an angel does not hover over a child. The child's name is not important now. The way she lived and died is. At age 10, this little girl lost her mother when she was killed in an argument over drugs. The girl went to New Jersey to live with her father, a man who sexually abused her. Then came several years of rough passage through New York City's foster care system. At 14, she was found dead. She had been battered, sexually molested, and left in the gutter of a New York suburb. Her body was not identified until late October, more than eight months after she had been found. "Her greatest fear," her friends said, "was that she would be unloved and nobody would notice if she was gone." Her fear turned out to be prophetic. One of her many foster parents said, "If someone had been there for this one, she might still be alive."

This is a very haunting "if" for me personally, as a leader of The Salvation Army. I ask myself, "What if we had been there for her? How much more would God have honored the expectation of our faith? What if a Sunday School class or an after–school program had been there for her?" Perhaps you might ask yourself, whatever your denomination, "What if I had spread my wings and hovered over this child?" Listen—can you hear the tolling of those bells of hell? They must be silenced.

My Story

My story is not dissimilar to this girl's story. The

abuse was different; it was more subtle because it was emotional. But it was abuse. Abuse comes in all kinds of guises. It is no respecter of persons; it touches rich and poor, dark–skinned and light–skinned, male and female. Its effects are always damaging.

My mother wasn't killed outright, but she was scarred by the effects of my father's alcohol abuse. He was a great guy when he wasn't drinking, but those times were very few. When under the influence of alcohol, he was verbally abusive. My mother and we kids were always the targets of that abuse. I died a thousand deaths emotionally during those early childhood days. My self–esteem was shattered in a thousand pieces. My young, immature mind could not sort out the differences between truth and alcohol–induced deceptions. I was gripped by an overwhelming sense of inferiority. I was confused and guilt–ridden. We lived in a working–class neighborhood, but we were poor because the paycheck always went to pay the tab at the corner liquor store. I wondered, "Am I to blame?" My mother was so unhappy all the time. I wondered, "Is it my fault?" I didn't dress like the other kids and my grooming left something to be desired. I wondered, "Why don't I measure up?" In order to get attention, I began to act out and misbehave. I didn't die, but my life was undeniably headed in the wrong direction. What if there had been no divine intervention? I can tell you with great confidence that the consequences would have been disastrous.

I thank God that someone was there for this one. Because there was a prize at stake, some friends invited me down the street to a Salvation Army Sunday School. A pastor, Ed Henderson, one of God's choice earth angels, spread his wings and took a personal interest in me. He saw potential in me that I was blind to—the rest is history. A few Sunday School teachers spread their wings over me along the way. What if they had not been there? The bells of hell were silenced in the shadow of their wings. By the way, my father stopped drinking when I made the decision to become a Salvation Army officer, and he was present for my commissioning (ordination). The prophetic promise voiced by Jeremiah is just as real today, if we "seek (work out God's plans) and pray."

I WONDER?

Their Stories

There were five children in Kathy's family and two functioning but alcoholic parents. The children's basic physical needs were met, but their emotional needs were not. In Bill's family, there were five children and two dysfunctional alcoholic parents. The children were often hungry and, at times, were placed in foster care.

In high school Kathy and Bill sought each other out and began to imitate life as they had experienced it. Married at ages 16 and 19, they soon found themselves overwhelmed with responsibility. Five children in five years, no high school diplomas, meager job skills and a propensity to addiction led them on a wild and dangerous chase—alcohol, drugs, bad companions, multiple jobs, fast cars, and motorcycles. They were trying to fill a void that they didn't even understand was there.

An elderly lady, an acquaintance from a brief attendance at the Lutheran church, asked if Kathy and Bill would permit her to take the three oldest children to Sunday School. Relieved to have this time away from the kids, Kathy and Bill agreed. The children always returned home happy—singing, clapping, and excited about their trips to Sunday School.

In due time Kathy and Bill discovered that the children were not attending Sunday School at the Lutheran church but at another church nearby. A pastor, Ray Wood, had begun faithfully picking them up and bringing them home every Sunday. One Sunday, he encountered Bill. Noting that there were three cars in the driveway, Ray invited Bill to bring the children to Sunday School himself and find out what they were experiencing. His response was, "I've tried church and it's not for me." But Ray persisted. Bill did give it a try, liked what he saw, and persuaded Kathy to accompany him the following week.

The young couple who were pastoring that church, Ray and his wife, Mary, took great care and patience to disciple the family; a year later they were all church members. Today Bill and Kathy Bentley are themselves pastoring a church in Toledo, Ohio. It is a fellowship specifically designed to reach out to the recovering community. And all because an elderly acquaintance and a young pastor couple made the decision to spread their wings and join the flight. What if they had not been there for Bill, Kathy, and their children? I wonder…

***

Vicki never saw her father and never knew her mother. Illegitimacy was her birthright. The last memory of her mother was a violent argument that occurred between her mother and grandparents when she was 3 years old. Her mother abruptly left that day, and Vicki began a new life with her grandparents. No one lived on that lonely, isolated farm in upstate New York except the three of them.

On some weekends, Vicki would go to stay with an aunt in a nearby town. The aunt took her to Sunday School. Vicki really liked the singing, the children, and the stories of Jesus, but it was a long way from the village to the farm, and she was able to attend only on special occasions.

There was, however, a single woman pastor, Beatrice Clinton, who made Vicki feel important and loved. Beatrice would occasionally drive all the way out to the farm to pick Vicki up for Sunday School, a distance of at least 15 miles each way. Vicki looked forward to those excursions with great eagerness and anticipation. That church became a place of refuge, and as she grew older, Vicki found herself totally immersed in all of its activities.

As a teenager Vicki was invited to work at the church's summer camp. The directors of the camp, David and Alice Baxendale, took a personal, pastoral interest in her. Later on, when Vicki was going through some difficult times and not attending church, they called her every Monday evening to see if she had gone to church the day before. Her response was always, "My church days are over, and you are wasting your time." However, because of the foundation that had already been laid in Vicki's life, the persistence of these pastors eventually paid off, and Vicki came back into the fold. The Baxendales invited her to live in their home while she was attending college. Vicki considers them "the parents that God gave me" and now, her own children call them Nana and Pop.

Today Vicki and her husband, "Gus," are in the ministry together. Vicki presently holds a very important leadership position in her church denomination. Nana and Pop are retired church leaders, David and Alice Baxendale. They, along with an aunt and pastor Beatrice Clinton, made the decision to spread their wings and join the flight for Vicki's future. What if they had not been there for her? I wonder…

***

In Don's family, there were seven children, an alcoholic father and a non–coping mother. His mother left when Don was nine, and he stayed with his father. When his father's alcoholism caused him to lose his job, Don was shipped, with all of his belongings in a pillowcase, back to his mother.

Don began to play in his junior high school band. One day the band leader said to the guy sitting next to Don in the horn section, "You play good because of that Salvation Army band you play in." This was enough motivation for Don; he decided that he needed to get into that band too.

Soon after that, young Don was running after a fire engine when he spied the Salvation Army building and decided that now would be the time to find out if someone there could teach him to play his horn better. The pastor, Major Martin Luther Cox, introduced him to the bandmaster, Kenneth Van Brunt, who told Don that he had to come to Sunday School for four weeks before he could join the band. So Sunday School it was for Don! He not only loved that experience, but soon he was playing in the band—and he became a better player in the junior high band too. He will tell you, unabashedly, that it was The Salvation Army that helped get him through those rough adolescent years.

After high school, he attended New York University at night. Later, while working, he went on to Columbia Graduate School, earned an M.A. in classics, then taught Greek and Latin at the college level for 10 years. Later, he went on to law school and became general counsel for General Electric, where he did mergers and acquisition work for 28 years. Today, retired from GE, he serves as the Salvation Army's area coordinator in Albany, N.Y. What if Major Martin Luther Cox and Bandmaster Kenneth Van Brunt had not spread their wings and joined the flight for Don's future? What if Sunday School had not been an alternative? Where would Don Ross be today? I wonder…

***

There were eight children in Pam's family and for years, they lived in an old abandoned junkyard school bus. At night the children slept huddled together for warmth on a pile of rags. Pam's father was a drinker, and her mother was mentally unstable. Violence and rage, parts of her mother's temperament, were always directed toward the children. Fear was Pam's constant companion; many nights she would cry herself to sleep. And each night would come the dream—of falling into a deep, swirling pit. She would always awake before hitting bottom.

When Pam was ten years old, her mother went to a local food pantry for help, and for some reason, Pam came along. While she waited for her mother, she met a nicely dressed little girl (in contrast to Pam, who was dirty and disheveled) named Lora. During the course of the conversation, Lora invited Pam to Sunday School. Pam's mother wasn't happy about the invitation and made it clear that Pam would have to find her own way there. Lora said that her dad, who was the pastor of the church, would be happy to pick Pam up. Sure enough, on the following Sunday, Clarence Kinnett made the five–mile trip in his the station wagon to pick Pam up at her home—the abandoned bus.

Pam's life began to change dramatically and take on new meaning. Lora became her first real friend. It wasn't long before Pam's four brothers and three sisters began to accompany her to Sunday School. They would be picked up earlier than the rest of the kids so they could be given a shower and clean clothes before the others arrived. Soon real cleansing began to take place on the inside as well.

At age 14, Pam was invited to live with a pastor couple, Paul and Jean Kelly, and their three small children, which meant moving to another state. But Pam agreed to go. The Kellys became her legal guardians and mentors. In high school, she became actively involved in clubs, choral groups, and church activities, and she graduated with honors.

Pam's life took many twists and turns after that, but today, she is an ordained minister serving as a missionary to Liberia. Paul and Jean Kelly, Pam's adopted parents, are now retired. They, along with Lora and her father, Clarence, made the decision to spread their wings and join the flight for Pam's future. What if they had not been there for her? I wonder…

***

Raymond was the youngest of eight children. He was born into a life of homelessness. Between the ages of 2 and 7, Raymond lived in 12 foster homes. These homes were not free from abuse. Raymond developed a severe stuttering problem, and his frequent address changes put him far behind educationally. These experiences took a tremendous toll on his self–image and feelings of self–worth.

Eventually Raymond was sent to live with a foster family who were Salvation Army officer/pastors. Before this time, Raymond had always been placed in the same home as his brother, Melvin, who was a year and a half older than Raymond. Problems and complications prevented this arrangement at that time.

Soon after, the pastor couple formally adopted Raymond, and his life took on new meaning and direction. It was in Sunday School where he first started to sing and found he could do so despite his speech impediment. Special education classes helped him catch up academically and speech therapy classes eventually cured his stuttering. Before long he was singing solos and performing numbers with the family musical ensemble. His confidence started to soar.

Today Raymond Livingston is happily married with a beautiful son. He works at the territorial headquarters of The Salvation Army in West Nyack, N.Y., and is principal vocal soloist for the Army's prestigious and world–renowned brass band, the New York Staff Band. A gifted singer, Raymond has been featured on several albums and CDs. And all because Raymond and Elizabeth Livingston made the decision to spread their wings and join the flight.

What if they had not been there for Raymond? What if Sunday School had not been there to awaken the gift within him. I wonder? Perhaps he would have followed in the same path as two of his brothers. Three years ago, Melvin (mentioned above), at age 28, hung himself in a small one–room apartment. For more than two weeks, no one noticed he was gone. Last year, another brother, age 33, attempted suicide and now lies in a coma in a special care facility. I wonder…

***

In her own words:

> *My name is Marilyn. When I saw the video 'Altars in the Street,' I choked and cried. I could've been one of those altars in the street. I also grew up in the streets of New York. My father, a heroin addict and wife beater and my mom unable to defend herself or us. Our world (my brother and I) was full of drugs, fights, scenes, tears, humiliation, and more.*
>
> *At the age of 8 years old, one of my mother's neighbors invited my brother and me to Sunday School at the Salvation Army. There*

I met pastor, Captain Gil Vega.... Captain Vega had a special and sincere love for the children. He did anything to get you to know Christ, like dramas, musicals, outings, mimes, I mean anything and everything... At one time we were over 50 teenagers not counting little kids. He had that special care for children that you have. He planted that seed in me...

Before going to this year's 'On the Edge' Conference [a young adult retreat], I was a little frustrated with the kids in my church [in Fajardo, Puerto Rico]. The pastor and I ended up being the only people working with them. Teaching Sunday School and Kid's Cell groups. These kids come from very poor neighborhoods, the poorest in the city, alcoholic parents, prostitute moms, drug addicted fathers and brothers, teenage pregnancy very common among them and illit-

eracy. You see, these kids nobody wants or could stand…

When I saw your video, the Lord confirmed what He had put in my heart before, and that is to keep working with the kids even if it is hard. He told me not to give up, because Captain Vega did not give up on me I should not give up on them. I could have been an altar in the streets of New York, but God did not allow the church to give up on me. The Sal [Salvation Army] was my family, a safe haven for my brother and me. Everything a child should receive and needs growing up I got from the church… I'm giving back to God what He gave me when I was a child, I'm truly grateful.

Marilyn Correa has spread her wings and is imitating life as it was imitated for her.

"Hope and a future" are common themes threading their way through these stories. The future has been made brighter for a fortunate few.

I am one of the fortunate few who have found help. Words are inadequate to express my gratitude. An earth angel brought light into my darkened world. An earth angel lighted one more dot on this darkened planet. An earth angel has made my future and my children's future much brighter.

Thank you! Thank you! Thank you!

The facts have been considered, the risks have been weighed, and now the decision must be made. What will it be? Will you lay this book down and go back to business as usual, or will you JOIN THE FLIGHT … for our future? If the latter is your choice, then read on as you continue to "seek and pray."

AN OUNCE OF PREVENTION IS WORTH…

Action Step 1: Re-establishing Priorities

The first step in seeking (working out) God's prosperity plan is to re–establish our priorities. The spiritual formation of our children must be at the top of our priority list. There is a little parable about the rescue of drowning persons from a rushing river that speaks to our priority. A rescuer is administering first aid to one when he spots another struggling person and pulls her out too. After a half dozen repetitions of this act, the rescuer starts running away while another floundering person is swept into view. "Aren't you going to rescue that fellow?" asks a bystander. "Heck no," shouts the rescuer, "I'm going upstream to find out what's pushing all these people in."

I have been upstream. This has been my passion and life's work for the past 40 years. I was pushed into that stream and I was one of the fortunate ones rescued. We need to "swim upstream" and challenge the "principalities and powers" that corrupt character. We need to promulgate a faith–based intervention and prevention program that will shape positive self–esteem and instill ethical, moral, and spiritual values for a healthy America. We cannot eliminate the shaping of spiritual values from this equation. Perhaps this is why so many programs fail.

Gandhi said, "If we are to teach real peace in this world and if we are to carry on a real war against war, we shall have to begin with children."

Harvard economist Richard Freeman found "that church attendance is a 'substantial' predictor of inner–city black males escaping poverty, drugs and crime."

David Myers, professor of psychology at Hope College, said, "And if religious communities are to advance America's renewal, they must begin by giving priority to the spiritual formation of their children."

Jesus said, "Let the little children come to Me, and do not forbid them; for of such is the kingdom of heaven."

Children must be reached during the formative years when they are receptive, adaptive, and malleable. As Martin Luther King said, we must "choose between chaos and community." William Booth said we must "build fences at the top of the cliff instead of having ambulances at the bottom."

I am saying we must revalue our children and reaffirm the future. We must put intervention and prevention at the top of our priority list.

There are some new intriguing statistics gathered in a survey by the Barna Research Group of Ventura, California. Based on a nationwide representative sampling, the survey data show that children between ages 5 and 13 have a 32% probability of accepting Christ as their Savior. Young people between the ages of 14 and 18 have just a 4% likelihood of doing so, while adults (ages 19 through death) have only a 6% probability of making that choice. The study also points out that children and adolescents are most impacted evangelistically by family members, peers, and their youth group (e.g. Sunday School, mid–week faith–based youth activities). In fact, the years prior to age 12 are when a majority of children make their decision as to whether or not they will follow Christ. The study clearly notes that the greatest window for evangelism currently available is among young children.

A 1999 study by Dr. Thom Rainer says that 4% of the Bridgers generation (those under 20) claim to be Christians. Yet a 1999 MTV statistic taken from a viewer poll indicated that 99% of their viewers (under 20) believe in a God. What a window of opportunity! God has given us a vision that will open this window wide. Prosperity, hope, and a future are just outside that window.

Action Step 2: A Return to Basics

The second step in seeking (working out) God's plan requires a return to the basics of Sunday School to provide spiritual formation in the 21st century. Several years ago I heard a radio interview with an international consultant on child delinquency (an American) who had just been the keynote speaker at an international symposium in the United Kingdom. I was driving at the time and could not write down the content of the interview verbatim, but I think I have captured its essence. The Duke of Edinburgh appeared at a gathering in London convened to draw attention to this growing problem. In the course of conversation he said to the consultant, "I suppose you have come to tell us how to solve all of our problems with the young people in the UK?" He replied, "Yes, I have, and I can do in two words." "Two words," said the Duke. "And what would they be?" "Sunday School," said the consultant. "The moral fabric of your society and mine is in decline because we have neglected Sunday School. Return to Sunday School and you will see a reversal in the trend that is demoralizing your country and mine."

Sunday School is in decline in America while poverty (spiritual as well as economic), neglect, and abuse are on the rise. We have produced a film titled "Altars in the Street" (mentioned in Marilyn's testimony earlier) to draw attention to this growing problem. It is designed to stir up a holy discontent with the way things are and inspire an expectation for the way things ought to be. It takes the parable of the rescuer and translates it into real life stories.

Make Hope Happen

This film is the focal piece of a 21st–century faith–based intervention/prevention initiative we are calling "HopeShare®." God has uniquely positioned and led me to be the initiator of this growing movement, one that has been divinely designed to make hope happen and reawaken God's "flight" plan—which includes plans "to prosper you ... plans for a hope and a future"—in the 21st century.

As part of HopeShare, we're offering a program that is time–tested, yet brand–new. We call it **SONday'SCOOL**®. It's Sunday School, but it's not. For one thing, it may not be on Sunday. And it's not just about sitting and listening. It's active ... It's alive ... It's cool! It's Sunday School with a twist, taking it out of the church basement and into real life. It's kids coming together throughout the week. It's adults sharing from their hearts. It's new life lessons learned. It's games ... food ... storytelling ... music ... friends ... excitement ... spread throughout the week. **SONday'SCOOL** is not just one program, but several. We have developed a menu of new, contemporary models and more.

This is more than just a one–hour–a–week program. What these children need is hope. They need a place to be safe, a place where they can learn to feel good about themselves and be good to others.

What these children need is a faith–based program of intervention and prevention, a program that is integrated into a community of caring people—making our programs and facilities (our homes, churches, community buildings, whatever?) an oasis in the middle of a parched, desolate and decaying world, a refuge in the midst of decadence that will bring safety, security, and hope.

Action Step 3: Getting Actively Involved

The third step in seeking (working out) God's plan is an action step. Get actively involved in the implementation of **SONday'SCOOL**. You can do this in one of five ways: Share this information with your pastor. Sponsor a **SONday'SCOOL** model in your home or neighborhood. Support a model or models by contributing financially. Volunteer your talent and time to a program. And finally, pray.

Action Step 4: Cultivate Care

We can take all of those steps. We can have the greatest program and teaching materials that have ever existed, but a curriculum without care is like a bed without its covers. It gives support but the warmth is not there. Without the warmth that bed will soon lose its attractiveness. Without the care, the curriculum will soon lose its attractiveness. In many ways I think the love and care is more important than the curriculum. The fourth, and probably most important step in seeking (working out) God's plan is to begin cultivating a caring spirit. And to this step I give the lion's share of space because this is the prescriptive counterpunch that will defeat Satan and his legions.

I think of Mrs. McFadden, who was one of a number of Sunday School teachers I had. She was not well educated and her teaching skills were inherited from the dark ages. We would take turns around the circle reading the portion of the lesson assigned. I knew that my turn was coming and concentrated on making sure I had all the words right. I was as oblivious to what the other kids were reading as they were to me when my turn came. As a teacher, on a scale of 1 to 10, Mrs. McFadden was probably a 1. Her classes were dull and boring.

But she was the finest Sunday School teacher I ever had. She made me feel important. She took a personal interest in me. When I missed a Sunday, there was a post card reminder in the mail followed by a telephone call and finally a visit to my home. She prayed for me, and I knew it. She remembered my birthday and other special occasions. She invited me to her Oceanside home during one summer vacation. She knew how to make me feel important and special. She went out of her way to take a special interest in me when I needed it most. There were not many who did during those days. I wouldn't have put up with me. She cared and it came across loud and clear!

Love Gives Lift

The power of love cannot be overestimated. Love is the power that fuels the flight. Without it we cannot become airborne. Without it the commitment will quickly dissipate. Without it the passion will soon lose its glow.

Art Linkletter learned this lesson almost accidentally. A financial sponsor of orphaned children around the world, he told the following story at a fund–raising event I was involved with.

> *I went to a home here in America to visit one of the children I was sponsoring. They told me that this little girl was a problem child and didn't mix well with the other children. She often acted out and was a difficult child to like. One day the children were playing out in the yard when one of the teachers observed this little girl placing an object up in the limb of a tree. The teacher thought to herself, "Aha! That little brat has stolen something and I've finally*

caught her" (even the teachers didn't like this little girl). She went to the tree and pulled out a piece of paper all rolled up. When she unrolled the paper there was a handwritten scribbled message that read, "To anyone who finds this, I love you."

What is the lesson in this story? That little girl wanted somebody to love her. She was looking for love. The financial sponsorship without love was powerless. The highly trained teacher without love was ineffective. The well–prepared curriculum without love was unproductive. Doug, the man who first took young Robert's interest in medicine seriously, would have been providing nothing but a "Band–aid®" had it not been for love. Dr. Beltran's interest, if he had not cared deeply, would have been short lived. Vi Brown's "gathering" would have dispersed quickly without love. Without love, Bob and Dorothy DeBolt's family would never have miraculously extended and thrived. Robert Muzikowski's baseball league, without love, wouldn't have gone beyond left field.

Love is the lift that will keep us soaring. Remember my earlier words? "We don't want to participate in the free fall. We want to participate in the 'free for all.'" It is the (love and) grace of God that is free for all and "lifts us out of the miry clay." It is the gift and lift of His (love and) grace that keeps us from falling. What the world needs now is love, sweet love. Care is cultivated through practice. Begin the cultivation process by extending that "angel antenna" on a regular basis. Will you "Come fly with me?"

A Difference?

Can one person make a difference? In my house there hangs a plaque with the following words written by Forest Witcraft:

> *A hundred years from now*
> *it will not matter*
> *what my bank account was,*
> *the sort of house I lived in,*
> *or the kind of car I drove—*
> *but the world may be different*

*because I was important
in the life of a child.*

Can one person make a difference? In Australia there is a beach where once a year starfish are washed up on its shores by the thousands. They are stranded there helpless where they will quickly bake in the hot sun and die. There is a proverbial story about a little boy walking down that beach, picking up starfish one by one and tossing them back into the sea. A bystander observing this act of compassion says to the boy, "Son, you're wasting your time. There are too many starfish and you will never begin to make a difference." The little boy picked up another starfish and tossing it into the water said, "Sir, it will make a difference to this one!"

Can one person make a difference? One by one we can change the world.

Do Something!

William Booth, co–founder of The Salvation Army, stood in the East End of London looking over a sea of helpless, lost, and dying humanity. He turned to his son, who was standing next to him, and said, "Bramwell, do something!" That compassionate command continues to resonate with great clarity today. May the following testimony prick your own conscience.

> *On the street I saw a small girl cold and shivering in a thin dress, with little hope of a decent meal. I became angry and said to God; 'Why did you permit this? Why don't you do something about it?' For a while God said nothing. That night He replied quite suddenly: 'I certainly did something about it … I made you.'*

Are you motivated to do something by putting your life on the line for a better future? Do you want to prosper and do you want the future to prosper through you? Hope Is an Angel … Join the Flight for Our Future and discover the plans He has for you—*plans to prosper you … plans to give you hope and a future.*

For more information on how you can become involved in this prosperity plan, go to...

www.jointheflight.com

Epilogue

I saw him in the church building for the first time on Wednesday. He was in his mid–70s, with thinning silver hair and a neat brown suit.

Many times in the past I had invited him to come to church. Several other Christian friends had talked to him about the Lord and had tried to share the good news with him.

He was a well–respected, honest man with so many characteristics a Christian should have, but he had never accepted Christ, nor entered the doors of a church.

'Have you ever been to a church service in your life?' I had asked him a few years ago. We had just finished a pleasant day of visiting and talking.

He hesitated. Then with a bitter smile he told me of his childhood experience some 60 years before.

He was one of many children in a large, impoverished family. His parents had struggled to provide food, with little left for housing and clothing.

When he was about 10, some neighbors invited him to worship with them. The Sunday School class had been very exciting.

He had never heard such songs and stories before! He had never heard anyone read from the Bible! After class was over, the teacher took him aside and said, 'Son, please don't come again dressed as you are now. We want to look our best when we come into God's house.'

He stood in his ragged, unpatched overalls. Then, looking down at his dirty, bare feet, he answered, 'No, ma'am, I won't—ever.' 'And I never did,' he said, abruptly ending our conversation.

Yes, I saw him in the church house for the first time on Wednesday. As I looked at that immaculately dressed old gentleman lying in the casket, I thought of the little boy of long ago. I could almost hear him say, 'No, Ma'am, I won't—ever.'

And I wept.

—Posted on the Internet, author unknown

Join the Flight...
for our future
with
SONday'SCOOL®

MAKE HOPE HAPPEN!
Order your FREE Startup Kit
Call 1-800-334-4431

(There may be a small handling & shipping charge in some instances.)

Those of us who have been through areas and neighborhoods that are dangerous, don't always consider that they are what many children call home.

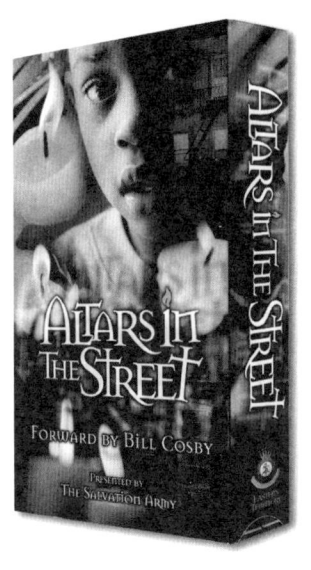

This poignant drama, filmed on location in some of America's roughest streets, tells the story of two children from different backgrounds.

To one of these children the intervention of people who dare to be involved (earth angels) means all the difference in the world. To the other it means the difference between life and death.

The film features a foreword by Bill Cosby and special music from singer Michael Tait, formerly of DC Talk.

MAKE HOPE HAPPEN!
Order Now
Call 1-800-334-4431

The Fringle Club has been created as a SON**day'**SCOOL model to develop value systems and ethical standards during the critical formative years when children are most impressionable and malleable (ages 3–6).

MAKE HOPE HAPPEN!
Order Now
Call 1-800-334-4431

Other Books by Joe Noland
"A Little Greatness"
"No Limits Together!"

Children's Book

By

Doris Noland

Musical CD

By

Doris Noland

Call 1-800-334-4431
To Order